THE BEATITUDES
BY
Arthur W. Pink

Contents

Introduction

Opinion has been much divided concerning the design, scope, and application of the Sermon on the Mount. Most commentators have seen in it an exposition of Christian ethics. Men such as the late Count Tolstoi have regarded it as the setting forth of a "golden rule" for all men to live by. Others have dwelt upon its dispensational bearings, insisting that it belongs not to the saints of the present dispensation but to believers within a future millennium. Two inspired statements, however, reveal its true scope. In Matthew 5:1, 2, we learn that Christ was here teaching His disciples. From Matthew 7:28, 29, it is clear that He was also addressing a great multitude of the people. Thus it is evident that this address of our Lord contains instruction both for believers and unbelievers alike.

It needs to be borne in mind that this sermon was Christ's first utterance to the general public, who had been reared in a defective Judaism. It was possibly His first discourse to the disciples, too. His design was not only to teach Christian ethics but to expose the errors of Pharisaism and to awaken the consciences of His legalistic hearers. In Matthew 5:20 He said, "Except your righteousness shall exceed the righteousness of the scribes and Pharisees, ye shall in no case enter into the Kingdom of heaven." Then, to the end of the chapter, He expounded the spirituality of the Law so as to arouse His hearers to see their need of His own perfect righteousness. It was their ignorance of the spirituality of the Law that was the real source of Pharisaism, for its leaders claimed to fulfill the Law in the outward letter. It was therefore our Lord's good purpose to awaken their consciences by enforcing the Law's true inner import and requirement.

It is to be noted that this Sermon on the Mount is recorded only in Matthew's Gospel. The differences between it and the Sermon on the Plain in Luke 6 are pronounced and numerous. While it is true that Matthew is by far the most Jewish of the four Gospels, yet we believe it is a serious mistake to limit its application to godly Jews, either of the past or the future. The opening verse of the Gospel, where Christ is presented in a twofold way, should warn us against such a restriction. There He is presented as Son of David and as Son of Abraham, "the father of all them that believe" (Rom. 4:11). Therefore, we are fully assured that this sermon enunciates spiritual principles that obtain in every age, and on this basis we shall proceed.

Christ's first preaching seems to have been summarized in one short but crucial sentence, like that of John the Baptist before Him: "Repent ye: for the Kingdom of heaven is at hand" (Matthew 3:2; 4:17). It is not appropriate in a brief study such as this to discuss that most interesting topic, the Kingdom of heaven—what it is and what the various periods of its development are—but these Beatitudes teach us much about those who belong to that Kingdom, and upon whom Christ pronounced its highest forms of benediction.

Christ came once in the flesh, and He is coming yet again. Each advent has a special object as connected with the Kingdom of heaven. The first advent of our Lord was for the purpose of establishing an empire among men and over men, by laying the foundations of that empire within individual souls. His second coming will be for the purpose of setting up that empire in glory. It is therefore vitally important that we understand what the character of the subjects in that Kingdom is, so that we may know whether we belong to the Kingdom ourselves, and whether its privileges, immunities, and future rewards are a part of our present and future inheritance. Thus one may grasp the importance of a devout and careful study of these Beatitudes. We must examine them as a whole; we cannot take one alone without losing a part of the lesson they jointly teach. These Beatitudes form one portrait. When an artist draws a picture, each line may be graceful and masterful, but it is the union of the lines that reveals their mutual relation; it is the combination of the various artistic delineations and minute touches that gives us the complete portrait. So here, though each separate aspect has its own peculiar beauty and grace and shows the hand of a master, it is only when we take all the lines in combination that we get the full portrait of a true subject and citizen in the Kingdom of God (Dr. A. T. Pierson paraphrased).

God's great salvation is free, "without money and without price" (Isa. 55:1). This is a most merciful provision of Divine grace, for were God to offer salvation for sale no poor sinner could secure it, seeing that he has nothing with which to purchase it. But the vast majority are insensible of this; yea, all of us are until the Holy Spirit opens our sin-blinded eyes. It is only those who have passed from death to life who become conscious of their poverty, take the place of beggars, are glad to receive Divine charity, and begin to seek the true riches. Thus "the poor have the Gospel preached to them" (Matthew 11:5), preached not only to their ears, but to their hearts!

Thus poverty of spirit, a consciousness of one's emptiness and need, results from the work of the Holy Spirit within the human heart. It issues from the painful discovery that all my righteousnesses are as filthy rags (Isa. 64:6). It follows my being awakened to the fact that my very best performances are unacceptable (yea, an abomination) to the thrice Holy One. Thus one who is poor in spirit realizes that he is a hell-deserving sinner.

Poverty of spirit may be viewed as the negative side of faith. It is that realization of one's utter worthlessness that precedes a laying hold of Christ by faith, a spiritual eating of His flesh and drinking of His blood (John 6:48-58). It is the work of the Spirit emptying the heart of self, that Christ may fill it. It is a sense of need and destitution. This first Beatitude, then, is foundational, describing a fundamental trait that is found in every regenerated soul. The one who is poor in spirit is nothing in his own eyes, and feels that his proper place is in the dust before God. He may, through false teaching or worldliness, leave that place, but God knows how to bring him back. And in His faithfulness and love He will do so, for the place of humble self-abasement before God is the place of blessing for His children. How to cultivate this God-honoring spirit is revealed by the Lord Jesus in Matthew 11:29.

He who is in possession of this poverty of spirit is pronounced blessed: because he now has a disposition that is the very reverse of that which was his by nature; because he possesses the first sure evidence that a Divine work of grace has been wrought within him; because such a spirit causes him to look outside of himself for true enrichment; because he is an heir of the Kingdom of heaven.

The First Beatitude

"Blessed are the poor in spirit: for theirs is the Kingdom of heaven"

Matthew 5:3

It is indeed blessed to mark how this sermon opens. Christ began not by pronouncing maledictions on the wicked, but by pronouncing benedictions on His people. How like Him was this, to whom judgment is a strange work (Isa. 28:21, 22; cf. John 1:17). But how strange is the next word: "blessed" or "happy" are the poor—"the poor in spirit." Who, previously, had ever regarded them as the blessed ones of earth? And who, outside believers, does so today? And how these opening words strike the keynote of all Christ's subsequent teaching: it is not what a man does but what he is that is most important.

"Blessed are the poor in spirit." What is poverty of spirit? It is the opposite of that haughty, self-assertive, and self-sufficient disposition that the world so much admires and praises. It is the very reverse of that independent and defiant attitude that refuses to bow to God, that determines to brave things out, and that says with Pharaoh, "Who is the Lord, that I should obey His voice?" (Ex. 5:2). To be poor in spirit is to realize that I have nothing, am nothing, and can do nothing, and have need of all things. Poverty of spirit is evident in a person when he is brought into the dust before God to acknowledge his utter helplessness. It is the first experiential evidence of a Divine work of grace within the soul, and corresponds to the initial awakening of the prodigal in the far country when he "began to be in want" (Luke 15:14).

The Second Beatitude

"Blessed are they that mourn, for they shall be comforted"

Matthew 5:4

Mourning is hateful and irksome to poor human nature. From suffering and sadness our spirits instinctively shrink. By nature we seek the society of the cheerful and joyous. Our text presents an anomaly to the unregenerate, yet it is sweet music to the ears of God's elect. If "blessed," why do they "mourn"? If they "mourn," how can they be "blessed"? Only the child of God has the key to this paradox. The more we ponder our text the more we are constrained to exclaim, "Never man spake like this Man!" "Blessed [happy] are they that mourn is an aphorism that is at complete variance with the world's logic. Men have in all places and in all ages regarded the prosperous and gay as the happy ones, but Christ pronounces happy those who are poor in spirit and who mourn.

Now it is obvious that it is not every species of mourning that is here referred to. There is a "sorrow of the world [that] worketh death" (2 Cor. 7:10). The mourning for which Christ promises comfort must be restricted to that which is spiritual. The mourning that is blessed is the result of a realization of God's holiness and goodness that issues in a sense of the depravity of our natures and the enormous guilt of our conduct. The mourning for which Christ promises Divine comfort is a sorrowing over our sins with a godly sorrow.

The eight Beatitudes are arranged in four pairs. Proof of this will be furnished as we proceed. The first of the series is the blessing that Christ pronounced upon those who are poor in spirit, which we took as a description of those who have been awakened to a sense of their own nothingness and emptiness. Now the transition from such poverty to mourning is easy to follow. In fact, mourning follows so closely that it is in reality poverty's companion.

The mourning that is here referred to is manifestly more than that of bereavement, affliction, or loss. It is mourning for sin.

It is mourning over the felt destitution of our spiritual state, and over the iniquities that have separated us and God; mourning over the very morality in which we have boasted, and the self-righteousness in which we have trusted; sorrow for rebellion against God, and hostility to His will; and such mourning always goes side by side with conscious poverty of spirit (Dr. Pierson).

A striking illustration and exemplification of the spirit upon which the Savior here pronounced His benediction is to be found in Luke 18:9-14. There a vivid contrast is presented to our view. First, we are shown a self-righteous Pharisee looking up toward God and saying, "God, I thank Thee that I am not as other men are, extortioners, unjust, adulterers, or even as this publican. I fast twice in the week, I give tithes of all that I possess. This may all have been true as he looked at it, yet this man went down to his house in a state of condemnation. His fine garments were rags, his white robes were filthy, though he knew it not. Then we are shown the publican, standing afar off, who, in the language of the Psalmist, was so troubled by his iniquities that he was not able to look up (Ps. 40:12). He dared not so much as lift up his eyes to heaven, but smote upon his breast. Conscious of the fountain of corruption within, he cried, "God be merciful to me a sinner." That man went down to his house justified, because he was poor in spirit and mourned for sin.

Here, then, are the first birthmarks of the children of God. He who has never come to be poor in spirit and has never known what it is to really mourn for sin, though he belong to a church or be an office-bearer in it, has neither seen nor entered the Kingdom of God. How thankful the Christian reader ought to be that the great God condescends to dwell in the humble and contrite heart! This is the wonderful promise made by God even in the Old Testament (by Him in whose sight the heavens are not clean, who cannot find in any temple that man has ever built for Him, however magnificent, a proper dwelling place—see Isa. 57:15 and 66:2)!

"Blessed are they that mourn." Though the primary reference is to that initial mourning commonly called conviction of sin, it is by no means to be limited to that. Mourning is ever a characteristic of the normal Christian state. There is much that the believer has to mourn over. The plague of his own heart makes him cry, "O wretched man that I am" (Rom. 7:24). The unbelief that "doth so easily beset us" (Heb. 12:1) and sins that we commit, which are more in number than the hairs of our head, are a continual grief to us. The barrenness and unprofitable-ness of our lives make us sigh and cry. Our propensity to wander from Christ, our lack of communion with Him, and the shallowness of our love for Him cause us to hang our harps upon the willows. But there are many other causes for mourning that assail Christian hearts: on every hand hypocritical religion that has a form of godliness while denying the power thereof (2 Tim. 3:5); the awful dishonor done to the truth of God by the false doctrines taught in countless pulpits; the divisions among the Lord's people; and strife between brethren. The combination of these provides occasion for continual sorrow of heart. The awful wickedness in the world, the despising of Christ, and untold human sufferings make us groan within ourselves. The closer the Christian lives to God, the more he will mourn over all that dishonors Him. This is the common experience of God's true people (Ps. 119:53; Jer. 13:17; 14:17; Ezek. 9:4).

"They shall be comforted." By these words Christ refers primarily to the removal of the guilt that burdens the conscience. This is accomplished by the Spirit's application of the Gospel of God's grace to one whom He has convicted of his dire need of a Savior. The result is a sense of free and full forgiveness through the merits of the atoning blood of Christ. This Divine comfort is "the peace of God, which passeth all understanding" (Phil. 4:7), filling the heart of the one who is now assured that he is "accepted in the Beloved" (Eph. 1:6). God wounds before healing, and abases before He exalts. First there is a revelation of His justice and holiness, then the making known of His mercy and grace.

The words "they shall be comforted" also receive a constant fulfillment in the experience of the Christian. Though he mourns his excuseless failures and confesses them to God, yet he is comforted by the assurance that the blood of Jesus Christ, God's Son, cleanses him from all sin (1 John 1:7). Though he groans over the dishonor done to God on every side, yet is he comforted by the knowledge that the day is rapidly approaching when Satan shall be cast into hell forever and when the saints shall reign with the Lord Jesus in "new heavens and a new earth, wherein dwelleth righteousness" (2 Peter 3:13). Though the chastening hand of the Lord is often laid upon him and though "no chastening for the present seemeth to be joyous, but grievous" (Heb. 12:11), nevertheless, he is consoled by the realization that this is all working out for him "a far more exceeding and eternal weight of glory" (2 Cor. 4:17). Like the Apostle Paul, the believer who is in communion with his Lord can say, "As sorrowful, yet alway rejoicing" (2 Cor. 6:10). He may often be called upon to drink of the bitter waters of Marah, but God has planted nearby a tree to sweeten them. Yes, mourning Christians are comforted even now by the Divine Comforter: by the ministrations of His servants, by encouraging words from fellow Christians, and (when these are not to hand) by the precious promises of the Word being brought home in power by the Spirit to their hearts out of the storehouse of their memories.

"They shall be comforted." The best wine is reserved for the last. "Weeping may endure for a night, but joy cometh in the morning" (Ps. 30:5). During the long night of His absence, believers have been called to fellowship with Him who was the Man of Sorrows. But it is written, "If... we suffer with Him.., we [shall] be also glorified together" (Rom. 8:17). What comfort and joy will be ours when shall dawn the morning without clouds! Then "sorrow and sighing shall flee away" (Isa. 35:10). Then shall be fulfilled the words of the great heavenly voice in Revelation 21:3, 4: Behold, the tabernacle of God is with men, and He will dwell with them, and they shall be His people, and God Himself shall be with them, and be their God. And God shall wipe away all tears from their eyes; and there shall be no more death, neither sorrow, nor crying, neither shall there be any more pain: for the former things are passed away.

The Third Beatitude

"Blessed are the meek: for they shall inherit the earth"

Matthew 5:5

There have been considerable differences of opinion as to the precise significance of the word meek. Some regard its meaning as patience, a spirit of resignation; some as unselfishness, a spirit of self-abnegation; others as gentleness, a spirit of non-retaliation, bearing afflictions quietly. Doubtless, there is a measure of truth in each of these definitions. Yet it appears to the writer that they hardly go deep enough, for they fail to take note of the order of this third Beatitude. Personally, we would define meekness as humility. "Blessed are the meek," that is, the humble, the lowly. Let us see if other passages bear this out.

The first time the word meek occurs in Scripture is in Numbers 12:3. Here the Spirit of God has pointed out a contrast from that which is recorded in the previous verses. There we read of Miriam and Aaron speaking against Moses: "Hath the Lord indeed spoken only by Moses? Hath He not spoken also by us?" Such language betrayed the pride and haughtiness of their hearts, their self-seeking and craving for honor. As the antithesis of this we read, "Now the man Moses was very meek." This must mean that he was actuated by a spirit the very opposite of the spirit of his brother and sister.

Moses was humble, lowly, and self-renouncing. This is recorded for our admiration and instruction in Hebrews 11:24-26. Moses turned his back on worldly honors and earthly riches, deliberately choosing the life of a pilgrim rather than that of a courtier. He chose the wilderness in preference to the palace. The humbleness of Moses is seen again when Jehovah first appeared to him in Midian and commissioned him to lead His people out of Egypt. "Who am I," he said, "that I should go unto Pharaoh, and that I should bring forth the children of Israel out of Egypt?" (Ex. 3:11). What lowliness these words breathe! Yes, Moses was very meek.

Other Scripture texts bear out, and seem to necessitate, the definition suggested above. "The meek will He guide in judgment: and the meek will He teach His way" (Ps. 25:9). What can this mean but that the humble and lowly-hearted are the ones whom God promises to counsel and instruct? "Behold, thy King cometh unto thee, meek, and sitting upon an ass" (Matthew 21:5). Here is meekness or lowliness incarnate. "Brethren, if a man be overtaken in a fault, ye which are spiritual, restore such an one in the spirit of meekness; considering thyself, lest thou also be tempted" (Gal. 6:1). Is it not plain that this means that a spirit of humility is required in him who would be used of God in restoring an erring brother? We are to learn of Christ, who was "meek and lowly in heart." The latter term explains the former. Note that they are linked together again in Ephesians 4:2, where the order is "lowliness and meekness." Here the order is deliberately reversed from that in Matthew 11:29. This shows us that they are synonymous terms.

Having thus sought to establish that meekness, in the Scriptures, signified humility and lowliness, let us now note how this is further borne out by the context and then endeavor to determine the manner in which such meekness finds expression. It must be steadily kept in mind that in these Beatitudes our Lord is describing the orderly development of God's work of grace as it is experientially realized in the soul. First, there is poverty of spirit: a sense of my insufficiency and nothingness. Next, there is mourning over my lost condition and sorrowing over the awfulness of my sins against God. Following this, in order of spiritual experience, is humbleness of soul.

The one in whom the Spirit of God has worked, producing a sense of nothingness and of need, is now brought into the dust before God. Speaking as one whom God used in the ministry of the Gospel, the Apostle Paul said, "The weapons of our warfare are not carnal, but mighty through God to the pulling down of strong holds; Casting down imaginations, and every high thing that exalteth itself against the knowledge of God, and bringing into captivity every thought to the obedience of Christ" (2 Cor. 10:4, 5). The weapons that the apostles used were the searching, condemning, humbling truths of Scripture. These, as applied effectually by the Spirit, were mighty to the pulling down of strongholds, that is, the powerful prejudices and self-righteous defenses within which sinful men took refuge. The results are the same today: proud imaginations or reasonings—the enmity of the carnal mind and the opposition of the newly regenerate mind concerning salvation is now brought into captivity to the obedience of Christ.

By nature every sinner is Pharisaical, desiring to be justified by the works of the Law. By nature we all inherit from our first parents the tendency to manufacture for ourselves a covering to hide our shame. By nature every member of the human race walks in the way of Cain, who sought to find acceptance with God on the ground of an offering produced by his own labors. In a word, we desire to gain a standing before God on the basis of personal merits; we wish to purchase salvation by our good deeds; we are anxious to win heaven by our own doings. God's way of salvation is too humbling to suit the carnal mind, for it removes all ground for boasting. It is therefore unacceptable to the proud heart of the unregenerate.

Man wants to have a hand in his salvation. To be told that God will receive nought from him, that salvation is solely a matter of Divine mercy, that eternal life is only for those who come empty-handed to receive it solely as a matter of charity, is offensive to the self-righteous religionist. But not so to the one who is poor in spirit and who mourns over his vile and wretched state. The very word mercy is music to his ears. Eternal life as God's free gift suits his poverty-stricken condition. Grace—the sovereign favor of God to the hell-deserving—is just what he feels he must have! Such a one no longer has any thought of justifying himself in his own eyes; all his haughty objections against God's benevolence are now silenced. He is glad to own himself a beggar and bow in the dust before God. Once, like Naaman, he rebelled against the humbling terms announced by God's servant; but now, like Naaman at the end, he is glad to dismount from his chariot of pride and take his place in the dust before the Lord.

It was when Naaman bowed before the humbling word of God's servant that he was healed of his leprosy. In the same way, when the sinner owns his worthlessness, Divine favor is shown to him. Such a one receives the Divine benediction: "Blessed are the meek." Speaking anticipatively through Isaiah, the Savior said, "The Lord hath anointed Me to preach good tidings unto the meek" (Isa. 61:1). And again it is written, "For the Lord taketh pleasure in His people: He will beautify the meek with salvation" (Ps. 149:4).

While humility of soul in bowing to God's way of salvation is the primary application of the third Beatitude, it must not be limited to that. Meekness is also an intrinsic aspect of the "fruit of the Spirit" that is wrought in and produced through the Christian (Gal. 5:22, 23). It is that quality of spirit that is found in one who has been schooled to mildness by discipline and suffering and brought into sweet resignation to the will of God. When in exercise, it is that grace in the believer that causes him to bear patiently insults and injuries, that makes him ready to be instructed and admonished by the least eminent of saints, that leads him to esteem others more highly than himself (Phil. 2:3), and that teaches him to ascribe all that is good in himself to the sovereign grace of God.

On the other hand, true meekness is not weakness. A striking proof of this is furnished in Acts 16:35-37. The apostles had been wrongfully beaten and cast into prison. On the next day the magistrates gave orders for their release, but Paul said to their agents, "Let them come themselves and fetch us out." God-given meekness can stand up for God-given rights. When one of the officers smote our Lord, He answered, "If I have spoken evil, bear witness of the evil: but if well, why smitest thou Me?" (John 18:23).

The spirit of meekness was perfectly exemplified only by the Lord Jesus Christ, who was "meek and lowly in heart." In His people this blessed spirit fluctuates, oftentimes beclouded by risings up of the flesh. Of Moses it is said, "They provoked his spirit, so that he spake unadvisedly with his lips" (Ps. 106:33). Ezekiel says of himself: "I went in bitterness, in the heat of my spirit; but the hand of the Lord was strong upon me" (Ezek. 3:14). Of Jonah, after his miraculous deliverance, we read: "It displeased Jonah exceedingly, and he was very angry (Jonah 4:1). Even the humble Barnabas parted from Paul in a bitter temper (Acts 15:37-39). What warnings are these! How much we need to learn of Christ!

"Blessed are the meek: for they shall inherit the earth." Our Lord was alluding to, and applying, Psalm 37:11. The promise seems to have both a literal and spiritual meaning: "The meek shall inherit the earth; and shall delight themselves in the abundance of peace." The meek are those who have the greatest enjoyment of the good things of the present life. Delivered from a greedy and grasping spirit, they are content with such things as they have. "A little that a righteous man hath is better than the riches of many wicked" (Ps. 37:16). Contentment of mind is one of the fruits of meekness of spirit. The proud and restless do not "inherit the earth," though they may own many acres of it. The humble Christian has far more enjoyment in a cottage than the wicked has in a palace. "Better is little with the fear of the Lord than great treasure and trouble therewith" (Prov. 15:16).

"The meek shall inherit the earth." As we have said, this third Beatitude is an allusion to Psalm 37:11. Most probably the Lord Jesus was using Old Testament language to express New Covenant truth. The flesh and blood of John 6:50-58 and the water of John 3:5 have, to the regenerate, a spiritual meaning; so here with the word earth or land. Both in Hebrew and in Creek, the principal terms rendered by our English words earth and land may be translated either literally or spiritually, depending upon the context.

His words, literally understood, are, "they shall inherit the land," i.e., Canaan, "the land of promise." He speaks of the blessings of the new economy in the language of Old Testament prophecy. Israel according to the flesh (the external people of God under the former economy) were a figure of Israel according to the spirit (the spiritual people of God under the new economy); and Canaan, the [earthly] inheritance of the former, is the type of that aggregate of heavenly and spiritual blessings which form the inheritance of the latter. To "inherit the land" is to enjoy the peculiar blessings of the people of God under the new economy; it is to become heirs of the world, heirs of God and joint-heirs with Christ [Rom. 8:17]. It is to be "blessed.., with all spiritual blessings in the heavenlies in Christ" [Eph. 1:3], to enjoy that true peace and rest of which Israel's in Canaan was a figure (Dr. John Brown).

No doubt there is also reference to the fact that the meek shall ultimately inherit the "new earth, wherein dwelleth righteousness" (2 Pet. 3:13).

The Fourth Beatitude

**"Blessed are they which do hunger and thirst
after righteousness. for they shall be filled"**

Matthew 5:6

In the first three Beatitudes we are called upon to witness the heart exercises of one who has been awakened by the Spirit of God. First, there is a sense of need, a realization of my nothingness and emptiness. Second, there is a judging of self, a consciousness of my guilt, and a sorrowing over my lost condition. Third, there is a cessation of seeking to justify myself before God, an abandonment of all pretenses to personal merit, and a taking of my place in the dust before God. Here, in the fourth Beatitude, the eye of the soul is turned away from self toward God for a very special reason: there is a longing after a righteousness that I urgently need but know that I do not possess.

There has been much needless quibbling as to the precise import of the word righteousness in our present text. The best way to ascertain its significance is to go back to the Old Testament Scriptures where this term is used, and then to shine upon these the brighter light furnished by the New Testament Epistles.

"Drop down, ye heavens, from above, and let the skies pour down righteousness: let the earth open, and let them bring forth salvation, and let righteousness spring up together; I the Lord have created it" (Isa. 45:8). The first half of this verse refers, in figurative language, to the advent of Christ to this earth; the second half to His resurrection, when He was "raised again for our justification" (Rom. 4:25). "Hearken unto Me, ye stouthearted, that are far from righteousness: I bring near My righteousness; it shall not be far off, and My salvation shall not tarry: and I will place salvation in Zion for Israel My glory" (Isa. 46:12, 13). "My righteousness is near; My salvation is gone forth, and Mine arms shall judge the people; the isles shall wait upon Me, and on Mine arm shall they trust" (Isa. 51:5). "Thus saith the Lord, Keep ye judgment, and do justice: for My salvation is near to come, and My righteousness to be revealed" (Isa. 56:1). "I will greatly rejoice in the Lord, my soul shall be joyful in my God; for He hath clothed me with the garments of salvation, He hath covered me with the robe of righteousness" (Isa. 61:10a). These passages make it clear that God's righteousness is synonymous with God's salvation.

The Scriptures cited above are unfolded in Paul's Epistle to the Romans, where the Gospel receives its fullest exposition. In Romans 1:16, 17a, Paul says, "For I am not ashamed of the Gospel of Christ: for it is the power of God unto salvation to every one that believeth; to the Jew first, and also to the Greek. For therein is the righteousness of God revealed from faith to faith." In Romans 3:22-24 we read, "Even the righteousness of God which is by faith of Jesus Christ unto all and upon all them that believe: for there is no difference: For all have sinned, and come short of the glory of God; Being justified freely by His grace through the redemption that is in Christ Jesus." In Romans 5:19, this blessed declaration is made: "For as by one man's disobedience many were made [legally constituted] sinners, so by the obedience of One shall many be made [legally constituted] righteous." In Romans 10:4, we learn that "Christ is the end of the Law for righteousness to every one that believeth."

The sinner is destitute of righteousness, for "there is none righteous, no, not one" (Rom. 3:10). God has, therefore, provided in Christ a perfect righteousness for each and all of His people. This righteousness, this satisfying of all the demands of God's holy Law against us, was worked out by our Substitute and Surety. This righteousness is now imputed to (that is, legally credited to the account of) the believing sinner. Just as the sins of God's people were all transferred to Christ, so His righteousness is placed upon them (2 Cor. 5:21). These few words are but a brief summary of the teaching of Scripture on this vital and blessed subject of the perfect righteousness that God requires of us and that is ours by faith in the Lord Christ.

"Blessed are they which do hunger and thirst after righteousness." Hungering and thirsting expresses vehement desire, of which the soul is acutely conscious. First, the Holy Spirit brings before the heart the holy requirements of God. He reveals to us His perfect standard, which He can never lower. He reminds us that except your righteousness shall exceed the righteousness of the scribes and Pharisees, ye shall in no case enter into the Kingdom of heaven" (Matthew 5:20). Second, the trembling soul, conscious of his own abject poverty and realizing his utter inability to measure up to God's requirements, sees no help in himself. This painful discovery causes him to mourn and groan. Have you done so? Third, the Holy Spirit then creates in the heart a deep "hunger and thirst" that causes the convicted sinner to look for relief and to seek a supply outside of himself. The believing eye is then directed to Christ, who is "THE LORD OUR RIGHTEOUSNESS" (Jer. 23:6).

Like the previous ones, this fourth Beatitude describes a twofold experience. It obviously refers to the initial hungering and thirsting that occurs before a sinner turns to Christ by faith. But it also refers to the continual longing that is perpetuated in the heart of every saved sinner until his dying day. Repeated exercises of this grace are felt at varying intervals. The one who longed to be saved by Christ, now yearns to be made like Him. Looked at in its widest aspect, this hungering and thirsting refers to a panting of the renewed heart after God (Ps. 42:1), a yearning for a closer walk with Him, and a longing for more perfect conformity to the image of His Son. It tells of those aspirations of the new nature for Divine blessing that alone can strengthen, sustain, and satisfy.

Our text presents such a paradox that it is evident that no carnal mind ever invented it. Can one who has been brought into vital union with Him who is the Bread of Life and in whom all fullness dwells be found still hungering and thirsting? Yes, such is the experience of the renewed heart. Mark carefully the tense of the verb: it is not "Blessed are they which have hungered and thirsted," but "Blessed are they which do hunger and thirst." Do you, dear reader? Or are you content with your attainments and satisfied with your condition? Hungering and thirsting after righteousness has always been the experience of God's true saints (Phil. 3:8-14).

"They shall be filled." Like the first part of our text, this also has a double fulfillment, both initial and continuous. When God creates a hunger and a thirst in the soul, it is so that He may satisfy them. When the poor sinner is made to feel his need for Christ, it is to the end that he may be drawn to Christ and led to embrace Him as his only righteousness before a holy God. He is delighted to confess Christ as his new-found righteousness and to glory in Him alone (1 Cor. 1:30, 31). Such a one, whom God now calls a "saint" (1

Cor. 1:2; 2 Cor. 1:1; Eph. 1:1; Phil. 1:1), is to experience an ongoing filling: not with wine, wherein is excess, but with the Spirit (Eph. 5:18). He is to be filled with the peace of God that passeth all understanding (Phil. 4:7). We who are trusting in the righteousness of Christ shall one day be filled with Divine blessing without any admixture of sorrow; we shall be filled with praise and thanksgiving to Him who wrought every work of love and obedience in us (Phil. 2:12, 13) as the visible fruit of His saving work in and for us. In this world, "He hath filled the hungry with good things" (Luke 1:53) such as this world can neither give to nor withhold from those who "seek the Lord (Ps. 34:10). He bestows such goodness and mercy upon us, who are the sheep of His pasture, that our cups run over (Ps. 23:5, 6). Yet all that we presently enjoy is but a mere foretaste of all that our "God hath prepared for them that love Him" (1 Cor. 2:9). In the eternal state, we will be filled with perfect holiness, for "we shall be like Him" (1 John 3:2). Then we shall be done with sin forever. Then we shall "hunger no more, neither thirst any more.

The Fifth Beatitude

"Blessed are the merciful: for they shall obtain mercy"

Matthew 5:7

In the first four Beatitudes, which have already been considered, a definite progression of spiritual awakening and transformation has been noted as one of the thrusts of our Lord's teaching. First, there is a discovery of the fact that I am nothing, have nothing, and can do nothing—poverty of spirit. Second, there is conviction of sin, a consciousness of guilt producing godly sorrow—mourning. Third, there is a renouncing of self-dependence and a taking of my place in the dust before God—meekness. Fourth, there follows an intense longing after Christ and His salvation—hungering and thirsting after righteousness. But, in a sense, all of this is simply negative, for it is the believing sinner's perception of what is defective in himself and a yearning for what is desirable. In the next four Beatitudes we come to the manifestation of positive good in the believer, the fruits of a new creation and the blessings of a transformed character. How this shows us, once more, the importance of noting that order in which God's truth is presented to us!

"Blessed are the merciful: for they shall obtain mercy." How grossly has this text been perverted by merit-mongers! Those who insist that the Bible teaches salvation by works appeal to this verse in support of their pernicious error. But nothing could be less to their purpose. Our Lord's purpose is not to set forth the foundation upon which the sinner's hope of mercy from God must rest, but rather it is to describe the character of His genuine disciples. Mercifulness is a prominent trait in this character. According to our Lord's teaching, mercy is an essential feature of that holy character to which God has inseparably connected the enjoyment of His own sovereign kindness. Thus, there is nothing whatever in this verse that favors the erroneous teachings of Roman Catholicism.

The position occupied by this Beatitude in its context is another key to its interpretation. The first four describe the initial exercises of heart in one who has been awakened by the Holy Spirit. In the preceding verse, the soul is seen hungering and thirsting after Christ, and then filled by Him. Here we are shown the first effects and evidences of this filling. Having obtained mercy of the Lord, the saved sinner now exercises mercy. It is not that God requires us to be merciful in order that we might be entitled to His mercy, for that would overthrow the whole scheme of Divine grace! But having been the recipient of His wondrous mercy, I cannot help but now act mercifully toward others.

What is mercifulness? It is a gracious disposition toward my fellow creatures and fellow Christians. It is that kindness and benevolence that feels the miseries of others. It is a spirit that regards with compassion the sufferings of the afflicted. It is that grace that causes one to deal leniently with an offender and to scorn the taking of revenge.

It is the forgiving spirit; it is the non-retaliating spirit; it is the spirit that gives up all attempt at self-vindication and would not return an injury for an injury, but rather good in the place of evil and love in the place of hatred. That is mercifulness. Mercy being received by the forgiven soul, that soul comes to appreciate the beauty of mercy, and yearns to exercise toward other offenders similar grace to that which is exercised towards one's self (Dr. A. T. Pierson).

The source of this merciful temper is not to be attributed to anything in our fallen human nature. It is true that there are some who make no profession of being Christians in whom we often see not a little of kindliness of disposition, sympathy for the suffering, and a readiness to forgive those who have wronged them. Admirable as this may be, from a purely human viewpoint, it falls far below that mercifulness upon which Christ here pronounced His benediction. The amiability of the flesh has no spiritual value, for its movements are neither regulated by the Scriptures nor exercised with any reference to the Divine authority. The mercifulness of this fifth Beatitude is that spontaneous outflow of a heart that is captivated by, and in love with, the mercy of God.

The mercifulness of our text is the product of the new nature implanted by the Holy Spirit in the child of God. It is called into exercise when we contemplate the wondrous grace, pity, and longsuffering of God toward such unworthy wretches as ourselves. The more I ponder God's sovereign mercy to me, the more I shall think of the unquenchable fire from which I have been delivered through the sufferings of the Lord Jesus. The more conscious I am of my indebtedness to Divine grace, the more mercifully I shall act toward those who wrong, injure, and hate me.

Mercifulness is one of the attributes of the spiritual nature that one receives at the new birth. Mercifulness in the child of God is but a reflection of the abundant mercy that is found in his heavenly Parent. Mercifulness is one of the natural and necessary consequences of a merciful Christ indwelling us. It may not always be exercised; it may at times be stifled or checked by fleshly indulgence. But when the general tenor of a Christian's character and the main trend of his life are taken into account, it is clear that mercifulness is an unmistakable trait of the new man. "The wicked borroweth, and payeth not again; but the righteous sheweth mercy, and giveth" (Ps. 37:21). It was mercy in Abraham, after he had been wronged by his nephew, that caused him to pursue and secure the deliverance of Lot (Gen. 14:1-16). It was mercy on the part of Joseph, after his brethren had so grievously mistreated him, that caused him to freely forgive them (Gen. 50:15-21). It was mercy in Moses, after Miriam had rebelled against him and the Lord had smitten her with leprosy, that caused him to cry, "Heal her now, O God, I beseech Thee" (Num. 12:13). It was mercy that caused David to spare the life of his enemy Saul when that wicked king was in his hands (1 Sam. 24:1-22; 26:1-25). In sad and striking contrast, of Judas it is said that he "remembered not to shew mercy, but persecuted the poor and needy man" (Ps. 109:16).

In Romans 12:8 the Apostle Paul gives vital instruction concerning the spirit in which mercy is to be exercised: "he that showeth mercy" is to do so "with cheerfulness." The direct reference here is to the giving of money for the support of poor brethren, but this loving principle really applies to all compassion shown to the afflicted. Mercy is to be exercised cheerfully, to demonstrate that it is not only done voluntarily but that it is also a pleasure. This spares the feelings of the one helped, and soothes the sorrows of the sufferer. It is this quality of cheerfulness that gives most value to the service rendered. The Greek word is most expressive, denoting joyful eagerness, a gladsome affability that makes the visitor like a sunbeam, warming the heart of the afflicted. Since Scripture tells us that "God loveth a cheerful giver" (2 Cor. 9:7), we may be sure that the Lord takes note of the spirit in which we respond to His admonitions.

"For they shall obtain mercy." These words enunciate a principle or law that God has ordained in His government over our lives here on earth. It is summarized in that well-known word: "Whatsoever a man soweth, that shall he also reap" (Gal. 6:Th). The Christian who is merciful in his dealings with others will receive merciful treatment at the hands of his fellows; for "with what measure ye meet, it shall be measured to you again" (Matthew 7:2). Therefore it is written, "He that followeth after righteousness and mercy findeth life, righteousness, and honour" (Prov. 21:21). The one who shows mercy to others gains personally thereby: "The merciful man doeth good to his own soul" (Prov. 11:17a). There is an inward satisfaction in the exercise of benevolence and pity to which the highest gratification of the selfish man is not to be compared. "He that hath mercy on the poor, happy is he" (Prov. 14:21b). The exercise of mercy is a source of satisfaction to God Himself: "He delighteth in mercy" (Micah 7:18). So must it be to us.

"For they shall obtain mercy." Not only does the merciful Christian gain by the happiness that accrues to his own soul through the exercise of this grace, not only will the Lord, in His overruling providence, make his mercifulness return again to him at the hands of his fellow men, but the Christian will also obtain mercy from God. This truth David declared: "With the merciful Thou wilt shew Thyself merciful" (Ps. 18:25). On the other hand, the Savior admonished His disciples with these words: "But if ye forgive not men their trespasses, neither will your Father forgive your trespasses" (Matthew 6:15).

"For they shall obtain mercy." Like the promises attached to the previous Beatitudes, this one also looks forward to the future for its final fulfillment. In 2 Timothy 1:16, 18, we find the Apostle Paul writing, "The Lord give mercy unto the house of Onesiphorus. . . . The Lord grant unto him that he may find mercy of the Lord in that day." In Jude 21, the saints are also exhorted to be "looking for the mercy of our Lord Jesus Christ"—this refers to the ultimate acknowledgement of us as His own redeemed people at His second coming in glory.

The Sixth Beatitude

"Blessed are the pure in heart: for they shall see God"

Matthew 5:8

This is another of the Beatitudes that has been grossly perverted by the enemies of the Lord, enemies who have, like their predecessors the Pharisees, posed as the champions of the truth and boasted of a sanctity superior to that which the true people of God would dare to claim. All through this Christian era, also, there have been poor, deluded souls who have claimed an entire purification of the old man. Others have insisted that God has so completely renewed them that the carnal nature has been eradicated, so that they not only commit no sins but have no sinful desires or thoughts. But the Spirit-inspired Apostle John declares, "If we say that we have [present tense] no sin, we deceive ourselves, and the truth is not in us" (1 John 1:8). Of course, such people appeal to the Scriptures in support of their vain delusion, applying to experience verses that describe the legal benefits of the Atonement. The words "and the blood of Jesus Christ His Son cleanseth us from all sin" (1 John 1:7) do not mean that our hearts have been washed from every trace of the corrupting defilements of evil, but primarily teach that the sacrifice of Christ has availed for the judicial blotting out of sins. When the Apostle Paul, describing the man who is a new creature in Christ, says that "old things are passed away; behold, all things are become new" (2 Cor. 5:17), he is speaking of the new disposition of the Christian's heart, which is wholly unlike his inner disposition prior to the Holy Spirit's work of regeneration.

That purity of heart does not mean sinlessness of life is clear from the inspired record of the history of God's saints. Noah got drunk; Abraham equivocated; Moses disobeyed God; Job cursed the day of his birth; Elijah fled in terror from Jezebel; Peter denied Christ. "Yes," perhaps someone will exclaim, "but all these things transpired before Christianity was established!" True, but it has also been the same since then. Where shall we go to find a Christian of superior attainments to those of the Apostle Paul? And what was his experience? Read Romans 7 and see. When he would do good, evil was present with him (v. 21). There was a law in his members, warring against the law of his mind, and bringing him into captivity to the law of sin that was in his members (v. 23). He did, with the mind, serve the Law of God; nevertheless, with the flesh he served the law of sin (v. 25). The truth is that one of the most conclusive evidences that we do possess a pure heart is the discovery and consciousness of the remaining impurity that continues to plague our hearts. But let us come closer to our text.

"Blessed are the pure in heart." In seeking an interpretation to any part of this Sermon on the Mount, the first thing to bear in mind is that those whom our Lord was addressing had been reared in Judaism. As one said who was deeply taught of the Spirit,

I cannot help thinking that our Lord, in using the terms before us, had a tacit reference to that character of external sanctity or purity which belonged to the Jewish people, and to that privilege of intercourse with God which was connected with that character. They were a people separated from the nations polluted with idolatry; set apart as holy to Jehovah; and, as a holy people, they were permitted to draw near to their God, the only living and true God, in the ordinances of His worship. On the possession of this character, and on the enjoyment of this privilege, the Jewish people plumed themselves.

A higher character, however, and a higher privilege, belonged to those who should be the subjects of the Messiah's reign. They should not only be externally holy, but "pure in heart"; and they should not merely be allowed to approach towards the holy place, where God's honour dwelt, but they should "see God," be introduced into the most intimate intercourse with Him. Thus viewed, as a description of the spiritual character and privileges of the subjects of the Messiah in contrast with the external character and privileges of the Jewish people, the passage before us is full of the most important and interesting truth (Dr. John Brown).

"Blessed are the pure in heart." Opinion is divided as to whether these words of Christ refer to the new heart received at regeneration or to that moral transformation of character that results from a Divine work of grace having been wrought in the soul. Probably both aspects of the truth are combined here. In view of the late place that this Beatitude occupies in the series, it would appear that the purity of heart upon which our Savior pronounced His blessing is that internal cleansing that both accompanies and follows the new birth. Thus, inasmuch as no inward purity exists in the natural man, that purity attributed by Christ to the godly man must be traced back, as to its beginnings, to the Spirit's sovereign work of regeneration.

The Psalmist said, "Behold, Thou desirest truth in the inward parts: and in the hidden part Thou shalt make me to know wisdom" (Ps. 51:6). This spiritual purity that God demands penetrates far beyond the mere outward renovations and reformations that comprise such a large part of the efforts now being put forth in Christendom! Much that we see around us is a hand religion—seeking salvation by works—or a head religion that rests satisfied with an orthodox creed. But God "looketh on the heart" (1 Sam. 16:7), that is, He looks upon the whole inner being, including the understanding, the affections, and the will. It is because God looks within that He must give a "new heart" (Ezek. 36:26) to His own people and blessed indeed are they who have received such, for it is a pure heart that is acceptable to the Giver.

As intimated above, we believe that this sixth Beatitude contemplates both the new heart received at regeneration and the transformation of character that follows God's work of grace in the soul. First, there is a "washing of regeneration" (Titus 3:5), by which we understand a cleansing of the affections, which are now subsequently set upon things above, instead of things below. This is closely linked with that change that follows upon the heels of regeneration, in which all believers undergo a "purifying [of] their hearts by faith" (Acts 15:9). Accompanying this is the cleaning of the conscience (Heb. 10:22), which refers to the removal of the burden of conscious guilt. This results in the inward realization that, "being justified by faith, we have peace with God through our Lord Jesus Christ" (Rom. 5:1).

But the purity of heart commended here by Christ goes further than this. What is purity? It is freedom from defilement and divided affections; it is sincerity, genuineness, and singleness of heart. As a quality of Christian character, we would define it as godly simplicity. It is the opposite of subtlety and duplicity. Genuine Christianity lays aside not only malice, but guile and hypocrisy also. It is not enough to be pure in words and in outward deportment. Purity of desires, motives, and intents is what should (and does in the main) characterize the child of God. Here, then, is a most important test for every professing Christian to apply to himself. Are my affections set upon things above? Are my motives pure? Why do I assemble with the Lord's people? Is it to be seen of men, or is it to meet with the Lord and to enjoy sweet communion with Him and His people?

"For they shall see God." Once more we would point out that the promises attached to these Beatitudes have both a present and a future fulfillment. The pure in heart possess spiritual discernment, and with the eyes of their understanding they obtain clear views of the Divine character and perceive the excellency of His attributes. When the eye is single the whole body is full of light.

In the truth, the faith of which purifies the heart, they "see God"; for what is that truth, but a manifestation of the glory of God in the face of Jesus Christ [2 Cor. 4:6]—an illustrious display of the combined radiance of Divine holiness and Divine benignity! . . . And he [who is pure in heart] not only obtains clear and satisfactory views of the Divine character, but he enjoys intimate and delightful communion with God. He is brought very near God: God's mind becomes his mind; God's will becomes his will; and his fellowship is truly with the Father and with His Son Jesus Christ.

They who are pure in heart "see God" in this way, even in the present world; and in the future state their knowledge of God will become far more extensive and their fellowship with Him far more intimate; for though, when compared with the privileges of a former dispensation, even now as with open face we behold the glory of the Lord [2 Cor. 3:18], yet, in reference to the privileges of a higher economy, we yet see but through a glass darkly— we know but in part, we enjoy but in part. But that which is in part shall be done away, and that which is perfect shall come. We shall yet see face to face and know even as we are known (1 Cor. 13:9-12); or to borrow the words of the Psalmist, we shall behold His face in righteousness, and shall be satisfied when we awake in His likeness (Ps. 17:15). Then, and not till then, will the full meaning of these words be understood, that the pure in heart shall see God (Dr. John Brown).

The Seventh Beatitude

"Blessed are the peacemakers: for they shall be called the children of God"

Matthew 5:9

This seventh Beatitude is the hardest of all to expound. The difficulty lies in determining the precise significance and scope of the word peacemakers. The Lord Jesus does not say, "Blessed are the peace-lovers," or "Blessed are the peace-keepers," but "Blessed are the peacemakers." Now it is apparent on the surface that what we have here is something more excellent than that love of concord and harmony, that hatred of strife and turmoil, that is sometimes found in the natural man, because the peacemakers that are here in view shall be called the children of God. Three things must guide us in seeking the true interpretation: (1) the character of those to whom our Lord was speaking; (2) the place occupied by our text in the series of Beatitudes; and (3) its connection with the Beatitude that follows.

The Jews, in general, regarded the Gentile nations with bitter contempt and hatred, and they expected that, under the Messiah, there should be an uninterrupted series of warlike attacks made on these nations, till they were completely destroyed or subjugated to the chosen people of God [an idea based, no doubt, on what they read in the Book of Joshua concerning the experiences of their forefathers]. In their estimation, those emphatically deserved the appellation of "happy" who should be employed under Messiah the Prince to avenge on the heathen nations all the wrongs these had done to Israel. How different is the spirit of the new economy! How beautifully does it accord with the angelic anthem which celebrated the nativity of its Founder: "Glory to God in the highest, and on earth peace, good will toward men!" (Dr. John Brown).

This seventh Beatitude has to do more with conduct than character, though, of necessity, there must first be a peaceable spirit before there will be active efforts put forth to make peace. Let it be remembered that in this first section of the Sermon on the Mount, the Lord Jesus is defining the character of those who are subjects and citizens in His Kingdom. First, He describes them in terms of the initial experiences of those in whom a Divine work is wrought. The first four Beatitudes, as has been previously stated, may be grouped together as setting forth the negative graces of their hearts. Christ's subjects are not self-sufficient, but consciously poor in spirit. They are not self-satisfied, but mourning because of their spiritual state. They are not self-important, not lowly or meek. They are not self-righteous, but hungering and thirsting for the righteousness of Another. In the next three Beatitudes, the Lord names their positive graces. Having tasted of the mercy of God, they are merciful in their dealings with others. Having received from the Spirit a spiritual nature, their eye is single to behold the glory of God. Having entered into the peace that Christ made by the blood of His cross, they are now anxious to be used by Him in bringing others to the enjoyment of such peace.

That which helps us, perhaps as much as anything else, to fix the meaning of this seventh Beatitude is the link that exists between it and the one that immediately follows. In our previous chapters, we have called attention to the fact that the Beatitudes are obviously grouped together in pairs. Poverty of spirit is always accompanied by mourning, as is meekness or lowliness by hungering and thirsting after the righteousness of God. Mercifulness toward men is united to purity of heart towards God, and peacemaking is coupled with being persecuted for righteousness' sake. Thus verses 10-12 supply us with the key to verse 9.

By approaching the seventh Beatitude from each of the three separate viewpoints mentioned above, we arrive at the same conclusion. First, let us consider the marked contrast between the tasks that God assigned to His people under the Old Covenant and New Covenant respectively. After the giving of the Law, Israel was commanded to take up the sword and to conquer the land of Canaan, destroying the enemies of Jehovah. The risen Christ has given different orders to His Church. Throughout this Gospel dispensation, we are to go into all nations as heralds of the cross, seeking the reconciliation of those who by nature are at enmity with our Master. Second, this grace of peacemaking supplements the six graces mentioned in the previous verses. Perhaps the fact that this is the seventh Beatitude indicates that it was our Lord's intent to teach that it is this attribute that gives completeness or wholeness to Christian character. We must certainly conclude that it is an unspeakable privilege to be sent forth as ambassadors of peace. Furthermore, those who fancy themselves to be Christians, yet have no interest in the salvation of fellow sinners, are self-deceived. They possess a defective Christianity, and have no right to expect to share in the blessed inheritance of the children of God. Third, there is a definite link between this matter of our being peacemakers and the persecution to which our Master alludes in verses 10-12. By mentioning these two aspects of

Christian character and experience side by side in His discourse, Christ is teaching that the opposition encountered by His disciples in the path of duty is the result of their faithfulness in the service to which they have been called. Thus we may be certain that the peacemaking of our text refers primarily to our being instruments in God's hands for the purpose of reconciling to Him those who are actively engaged in warfare against Him (cf. John 15:17-27).

We have dealt at some length on the reasons that have led us to conclude that the peacemakers referred to in our text are those who beseech sinners to be reconciled to God (2 Cor. 5:20), because most of the commentators are very unsatisfactory in their expositions. They see in this Beatitude nothing more than a blessing pronounced by Christ on those who endeavor to promote unity, to heal breaches, and to restore those who are estranged. While we fully agree that this is a most blessed exercise, and that the Christian is, by virtue of his being indwelt by Christ, a lover of peace and concord, yet we do not believe that this is what our Lord had in mind here.

The believer in Christ knows that there is no peace for the wicked. Therefore, he earnestly desires that they should acquaint themselves with God and be at peace (Job 22:21). Believers know that peace with God is only through our Lord Jesus Christ (Col. 1:19, 20). For this reason we speak of Him to our fellow men as the Holy Spirit leads us to do so. Our feet are "shod with the preparation of the Gospel of peace" (Eph. 6:15); thus we are equipped to testify to others concerning the grace of God. Of us it is said, "How beautiful are the feet of them that preach the Gospel of peace, and bring glad tidings of good things!" (Rom. 10:15). All such are pronounced blessed by our Lord. They cannot but be blessed. Next to the enjoyment of peace in our own souls must be our delight in bringing others also (by God's grace) to enter into this peace. In its wider application, this word of Christ may also refer to that spirit in His followers that delights to pour oil upon the troubled waters, that aims to right wrongs, that seeks to restore kindly relations by dealing with and removing difficulties and by neutralizing and silencing acrimonies.

"Blessed are the peacemakers: for they shall be called the children of God." The word called here seems to mean "acknowledged as." God shall own them as His own children.

He is "the God of peace" (Heb. 13:20). His great object, in the wonderful scheme of redemption, is to "gather together in one all things in Christ," whether they be things "in heaven," or things "on earth" (Eph. 1:10). And all those who, under the influence of Christian truth, are peacemakers show that they are animated with the same principle of action as God, and as "obedient children" [1 Pet. 1:14] are cooperating with Him in His benevolent design (Dr. John Brown).

The world may despise them as fanatics, professors of religion may regard them as narrow-minded sectarians, and their relatives may look upon them as fools. But the great God owns them as His children even now, distinguishing them by tokens of His peculiar regard and causing His Spirit within them to witness to them that they are sons of God. But in the Day to come, He will publicly avow His relationship to them in the presence of an assembled universe. However humble their present situation in life may be, however despised and misrepresented by their fellow men, they shall yet "shine forth as the sun in the Kingdom of their Father" (Matthew 13:43). Then shall transpire the glorious and long-awaited "manifestation of the sons of God" (Rom. 8:19).

The Eighth Beatitude

"Blessed are they which are persecuted for righteousness' sake: for theirs is the Kingdom of heaven. Blessed are ye, when men shall revile you, and persecute you, and shall say all manner of evil against you falsely, for My sake. Rejoice, and be exceeding glad: for great is your reward in heaven: for so persecuted they the prophets which were before you"

Matthew 5:10-12

The Christian life is full of strange paradoxes that are quite insoluble to human reason, but that are easily understood by the spiritual mind. God's saints rejoice with joy unspeakable, yet they also mourn with a lamentation to which the worldling is an utter stranger. The believer in Christ has been brought into contact with a source of vital satisfaction that is capable of meeting every longing, yet he pants with a yearning like that of a thirsty heart (Ps. 42:1). He sings and makes melody in his heart to the Lord, yet he groans deeply and daily. His experience is often painful and perplexing, yet he would not part with it for all the gold in the world. These puzzling paradoxes are among the evidences he possesses that he is indeed blessed of God. Such are the thoughts evoked by our present text. Who, by mere reasoning, would ever conclude that the reviled, the persecuted, the defamed, are blessed?

It is a strong proof of human depravity that men's curses and Christ's blessings should meet on the same persons. Who would have thought that a man could be persecuted and reviled, and have all manner of evil said of him, for righteousness' sake? And do wicked men really hate justice and love those who defraud and wrong their neighbours? No; they do not dislike righteousness as it respects themselves: it is only that species of it which respects God and religion that excites their hatred. If Christians were content with doing justly and loving mercy, and would cease walking humbly with God [Micah 6:8], they might go through the world, not only in peace, but with applause; but he that will live godly in Christ Jesus shall suffer persecution (2 Tim. 3:12). Such a life reproves the ungodliness of men and provokes their resentment (Andrew Fuller).

Verses 10-12 plainly go together and form the eighth and last Beatitude of this series. It pronounces a double blessing upon a double line of conduct. This at once suggests that it is to be looked at in a twofold way. What we have in verse 10 is to be regarded as an appendix to the whole series, describing the experience that will surely be met with by those whose character Christ has described in the previous verses. The carnal mind is enmity against God (Rom. 8:7), and the more His children are conformed to His image the more they will bring down upon themselves the spite of His foes. Being "persecuted for righteousness' sake" means being opposed because of right living. Those who perform their Christian duty condemn those who live to please self, and therefore evoke their hatred. This persecution assumes various forms, from annoying and taunting to oppressing and tormenting.

Verses 10-12 contain a supplementary word to the seventh Beatitude. That which arouses the anger of Satan and most stirs up his children are the efforts of Christians to be peacemakers. The Lord here prepares us to expect that loyalty to Him and His Gospel will result in our own peace being disturbed, introducing us to the prospect of strife and warfare. Proof of this is found when He says, "For so persecuted they the prophets which were before you." It is service for God that calls forth the fiercest opposition. Necessarily so, for we are living in a world that is hostile to Christ, as His cross has once and for all demonstrated.

Our Lord mentions, in verse 11, three sorts of suffering that His disciples should expect to endure in the line of duty. The first is reviling, that is, verbal abuse or vituperation. The second is persecution. This word is a proper rendering of a Greek word meaning "to pursue, which means, in this case, "to harass, trouble, or molest" (either physically or verbally). It may include the sort of handling or hunting down to which Saul of Tarsus subjected the Church before he was apprehended by Christ (Acts 8, 9). Christ sets forth the third type of suffering as follows: "Blessed are ye, when men. . . shall say all manner of evil against you falsely. . . ." Thus He describes the defamation of character to which His saints must he subjected.

This last is doubly painful to sensitive temperaments, finding its realization in the countless calumnies that the Devil is never weary of inventing in order to intensify the sufferings of the children of God. The words "persecuted for righteousness' sake" and "for My sake" caution us to see to it that we are opposed and hated solely because we are the followers of the Lord Jesus, and not on account of our own misconduct or injudicious behavior (see 1 Pet. 2:19-24).

Persecution has ever been the lot of God's people. Cain slew Abel. "And wherefore slew he him? Because his own works were evil, and his brother's righteous" (1 John 3:12). Joseph was persecuted by his brethren, and down in Egypt he was cast into prison for righteousness' sake (Gen. 37, 39). Moses was reviled again and again (see Ex. 5:21; 14:11; 16:2; 17:2; etc.). Samuel was rejected (1 Sam. 8:5). Elijah was despised (1 Kings 18:17) and persecuted (1 Kings 19:2). Micaiah was hated (I Kings 22:8). Nehemiah was oppressed and defamed (Neh. 4). The Savior Himself, the faithful Witness of God, was put to death by the people to whom He ministered. Stephen was stoned, Peter and John cast into prison, James beheaded, while the entire course of the Apostle Paul's Christian life and ministry was one long series of bitter and relentless persecutions.

It is true that the persecution of the saints today is in a much milder form than it assumed in other ages. Nevertheless, it is just as real. Through the goodness of God we have long been protected from legal persecution, but the enmity of Satan finds other ways and means of expressing itself. Let persecuted Christians remember this comforting truth: "For unto you it is given in the behalf of Christ, not only to believe on Him, but also to suffer for His sake" (Phil. 1:29). The words of Christ in John 15:19, 20, have never been repealed:

If ye were of the world, the world would love his own: but because ye are not of the world, but I have chosen you out of the world, therefore the world hateth you. Remember the word that I said unto you, The servant is not greater than his lord. If they have persecuted Me, they will also persecute you; if they have kept My saying, they will keep yours also.

The world's hatred manifests itself in derision, reproach, slander, and ostracism. May Divine grace enable us to heed this word: "But if, when ye do well, and suffer for it, yet take it patiently, this is acceptable with God" (1 Pet. 2:20).

The Lord Jesus here pronounced blessed or happy those who, through devotion to Him, would be called upon to suffer. They are blessed because such are given the unspeakable privilege of having fellowship in the sufferings of the Savior (Phil. 3:10). They are blessed because such "tribulation worketh patience; And patience, experience; and experience, hope: And hope maketh not ashamed" (Rom. 5:3-5). They are blessed because they shall be fully recompensed in the great Day to come. Here is rich comfort indeed. Let not the soldier of the cross be dismayed because the fiery darts of the wicked one are hurled against him. Rather let him gird on more firmly the Divinely provided armor. Let not the child of God become discouraged because his efforts to please Christ make some of those who call themselves Christians speak evil of him. Let not the Christian imagine that fiery trials are an evidence of God's disapproval.

"Rejoice, and be exceeding glad." Not only are the afflictions that faithfulness to Christ involves to be patiently endured, but they are to be received with joy and gladness. This we should do for three reasons. (1) These afflictions come upon us for Christ's sake; and since He suffered so much for our redemption, we ought to rejoice greatly when we are called upon to suffer a little for Him.(2) These trials bring us into fellowship with a noble company of martyrs, for to meet with afflictions associates us with the holy prophets and apostles. In such company, reproach becomes praise and dishonor turns to glory. (3) We who suffer persecution for Christ's sake are promised a great reward in heaven. Verily, we may rejoice, however fierce the present conflict may be. Having deliberately chosen to suffer with Christ rather than enjoy the pleasures of sin for a season (Heb. 11:25), we shall also reign with Him, according to His own sure promise (Rom. 8:17). Remember Peter and John, who "departed from the presence of the council, rejoicing that they were counted worthy to suffer shame for His name" (Acts 5:41). So, too, Paul and Silas, in the Philippian dungeon and with backs bleeding, "sang praises unto God" (Acts 16:25). We are told that others "took joyfully the spoiling of [their] goods," knowing in themselves that they had "in heaven a better and an enduring substance" (Heb. 10:34). May Divine grace enable all maligned, misunderstood, and oppressed saints of God to draw from these precious words of Christ that comfort and strength that they need.

Conclusion-The Beatitudes and Christ

Our meditations upon the Beatitudes would not be complete unless they turned our thoughts to the Person of our blessed Lord. As we have endeavored to show, they describe the character and conduct of a Christian. Since Christian character is formed in us by the experiential process of our being conformed to the image of God's Son, then we must turn our gaze upon Him who is the perfect pattern. In the Lord Jesus Christ we find the brightest manifestations and the highest exemplifications of all the various spiritual graces that are found (as dim reflections) in His followers. Not one or two but all of these perfections were displayed by Him, for He is not only lovely, but "altogether lovely" (Song of Sol. 5:16). May the Holy Spirit, who is here to glorify Him, take now of the things of Christ and show them unto us (John 16:14, 15).

First let us consider the words, "Blessed are the poor in spirit." How marvelous it is to see how the Scriptures speak of Him who was rich becoming poor for our sakes, that we through His poverty might be rich (2 Cor. 8:9). Great indeed was the poverty into which He entered. Born of parents who were poor in this world's goods, He commenced His earthly life in a manger. During His youth and early manhood, He toiled at the carpenter's bench. After His public ministry had begun, He declared that though the foxes had their holes and the birds of the air their nests, the Son of Man had not where to lay His head (Luke 9:58). If we trace out the Messianic utterances recorded in the Psalms by the Spirit of prophecy, we shall find that again and again He confessed to God His poverty of spirit: "I am poor and sorrowful" (Ps. 69:29); "Bow down Thine ear, O Lord, hear Me: for I am poor and needy" (Ps. 86:1); "For I am poor and needy, and My heart is wounded within Me" (Ps. 109:22).

Second, let us ponder the words, "Blessed are they that mourn." Christ was indeed the chief Mourner. Old Testament prophecy contemplated Him as "a Man of Sorrows, and acquainted with grief" (Isa. 53:3). When contending with the Pharisees over their slavish observance of the Sabbath, and while seeking to teach them, by precept and example, a proper understanding of God's holy institution, He "grieved for the hardness of their hearts" (Mark 3:5). Behold Him sighing before He healed the deaf and dumb man (Mark 7:34). Mark Him weeping by the graveside of Lazarus (John 11:35). Hear His lamentation over the beloved city: "O Jerusalem, Jerusalem... how often would I have gathered thy children together" (Matthew 23:37). Draw near and reverently behold Him in the gloom of Gethsemane, pouring out His petitions to the Father "with strong crying and tears" (Heb. 5:7). Bow down in awe and wonder as you hear Him crying from the cross, "My God, My God, Why hast Thou forsaken Me?" (Mark 15:34). Hearken to His plaintive plea, "Is it nothing to you, all ye that pass by? behold, and see if there be any sorrow like unto My sorrow" (Lam. 1:12).

Third, behold the beauty of Christ in the saying, "Blessed are the meek." A score of examples might be drawn from the Gospels that illustrate the lovely lowliness of the incarnate Lord of glory. Mark it in the men selected by Him to be His ambassadors. He chose not the wise, the learned, the great, or the noble. At least four of them were fishermen, and one was in the employment of the Roman government as a despised tax collector. Witness His lowliness in the company that He kept. He sought not the rich and renowned, but was "a friend of publicans and sinners" (Matthew 11:19). See it in the miracles that He wrought. Again and again He enjoined the healed to go and tell no man what had been done for them. Behold it in the unobtrusiveness of His service. Unlike the hypocrites, who sounded a trumpet before them when they were about to bestow alms on some poor person, He sought not the limelight, but shunned advertising and disdained popularity. When the crowds would make Him their idol, He avoided them (Mark 1:45; 7:24). "When Jesus therefore perceived that they would come and take Him by force, to make Him a king, He departed again into a mountain Himself alone" (John 6:15). When His brethren urged Him, saying, "Shew Thyself to the world," He declined and went up to the feast in secret (John 7:2-10). When He, in fulfillment of prophecy, presented Himself to Israel as their King, He entered Jerusalem in a most lowly fashion, riding upon the foal of an ass (Zech. 9:9; John 12:14).

Fourth, consider how these words are best exemplified in Christ: "Blessed are they which do hunger and thirst after righteousness." What a summary this is of the inner life of the man Christ Jesus! Before the Incarnation, the Holy Spirit announced, "And righteousness shall be the girdle of His loins" (Isa. 11:5). When Christ entered this world, He said, "Lo, I come to do Thy will, O God" (Heb. 10:9). As a boy of twelve He asked, "Wist ye not that I must be about My Father's business?" (Luke 2:49). At the beginning of His public ministry He declared, "Think not that I am come to destroy the law, or the prophets: I am not come to destroy, but to fulfill" (Matthew 5:17). To His disciples He declared, "My meat is to do the will of Him that sent Me, and to finish His work" (John 4:34). Of Him the Holy Spirit has said, "Thou lovest righteousness, and hatest wickedness: therefore God, Thy God, hath anointed Thee with the oil of gladness above Thy fellows" (Ps. 45:7). Well may He be called "THE LORD OUR RIGHTEOUSNESS" (Jer. 23:6).

Fifth, note the words, "Blessed are the merciful." In Christ we see mercy personified. It was mercy to poor lost sinners that caused the Son of God to exchange the glory of heaven for the shame of earth. It was wondrous and matchless mercy that took Him to the cross, there to be made a curse for His people. So, it is "not by works of righteousness which we have done, but according to His mercy [that] He saved us" (Titus 3:5). He is, even now, exercising mercy on our behalf as our "merciful and faithful High Priest" (Heb. 2:17). So also we are continually to be "looking for the mercy of our Lord Jesus Christ unto eternal life" (Jude 21). because He will show mercy in the Day of Judgment to all who believe upon Him (II Tim. 1:18).

Sixth, contemplate the words, "Blessed are the pure in heart." This, too, was perfectly exemplified in Christ. He was the "Lamb without blemish and without spot (1 Pet. 1:19). In becoming man, He was uncontaminated, contracting none of the defilements of sin. His humanity was, and is, perfectly holy (Luke 1:35). He was "holy, harmless, undefiled, separate from sinners" (Heb. 7:26). "In Him is no sin" (1 John 3:5). Therefore, He "did no sin" (1 Pet. 2:22) and "knew no sin" (2 Cor. 5:21). "He is pure" (1 John 3:3). Because He was absolutely pure in nature, His motives and actions were always pure. When He said, "I seek not Mine own glory" (John 8:50), He summed up the whole of His earthly career.

Seventh, ponder the words, "Blessed are the peacemakers." Supremely true is this of our blessed Savior. He is the One who "made peace through the blood of His cross" (Col. 1:20). He was appointed to be a propitiation (Rom. 3:25), that is, the One who would appease God's wrath, satisfying every demand of His broken Law, and glorifying His justice and holiness. He has also made peace between Jews and Gentiles (Eph. 2:11-18). Even now Christ Jesus is seated in majesty upon the throne of His father David (Acts 2:29-36), reigning as the "Prince of Peace. Of the increase of His government and peace there shall be no end, upon the throne of David" (Isa. 9:6, 7). When Christ returns to raise the dead and to judge the world in righteousness, then He shall purge this war-torn earth of sin and of all the effects of the Fall (Rom. 8:19-23). We may look confidently to that time when the Lord Christ shall thus restore peace in the "new heavens and a new earth, wherein dwelleth righteousness" (2 Pet. 3:13).

Eighth, meditate on these words: "Blessed are they which are persecuted for righteousness' sake." None was ever persecuted as was the Righteous One, as may be seen by the symbolic reference to Him in Revelation 12:4! By the Spirit of prophecy He declared, "I am afflicted and ready to die from My youth up" (Ps. 88:15). At the beginning of His ministry, when Jesus was teaching in Nazareth (His home town), the people "rose up, and thrust Him out of the city, and led Him unto the brow of the hill whereon their city was built, that they might cast Him down headlong" (Luke 4:29). In the temple precincts, leaders of the Jews "took up stones to cast at Him" (John 8:59). All through His ministry His steps were dogged by enemies. The religious leaders charged Him with having a demon (John 8:48). Those who sat in the gate spoke against Him, and He was the song of the drunkards (Ps. 69:12). At His trial they plucked off His hair (Isa. 50:6), spat in His face, buffeted Him, and smote Him with the palms of their hands (Matthew 26:67). After He was scourged by the soldiers and crowned with thorns, He was led carrying His own cross to Calvary, where they crucified Him. Even in His dying hours He was not left in peace, but was persecuted by revilings and scoffings. How unutterably mild, by comparison, is the persecution that we are called upon to endure for His sake!

In like manner, each of the promises attached to the Beatitudes finds its accomplishment in Christ. Poor in spirit He was, and His supremely is the Kingdom. Mourn He did, yet He will be comforted as He sees of the travail of His soul (Isa. 53:11). He was meekness personified, yet He is now seated upon a throne of glory. He hungered and thirsted after righteousness, yet now He is filled with satisfaction as He beholds that the righteousness which He worked out has been imputed to His people. Pure in heart, He sees God as none other sees him (Matthew 11:27). As the Peacemaker, He is acknowledged as the unique Son of God by all the blood-bought children. As the persecuted One, great is His reward, for He has been given the name above all others (Phil. 2:9-11). May the Spirit of God occupy us more and more with Him who is fairer than the children of men (Ps. 45:2).

Made in the USA
Lexington, KY
18 January 2017